Also by John Updike

AMERICANA

John Updike

AMERICANA
and Other Poems

Alfred A. Knopf · *New York*
2001

ACKNOWLEDGMENTS

Some of these poems were previously published in *The New Republic*, *The Atlantic Monthly*, *The American Scholar*, *Poetry*, *The American Poetry Review*, *Ontario Review*, *The Paris Review*, *Partisan Review*, *The Georgia Review*, *The Yale Review*, *Bostonia*, *River City*, *The Formalist*, *DoubleTake*, *Literal Latté*, and *The Boston Phoenix*. The following first appeared in *The New Yorker*: "Island Cities," "Before the Mirror," "The Hedge," "Upon Becoming a Senior Citizen," "Ocular Hypertension," "Radiators," "Montes Veneris," and "Jesus and Elvis." Translated into Portuguese, "A Brazilian Valentine" was one of several valentines printed in the newspaper *Folha de São Paulo*. "Americana," under the title (now its subtitle) "Poem Begun on Thursday, October 14, 1993, at O'Hare Airport, Terminal 3, around Six O'Clock P.M.," was first published as a broadside by The Literary Renaissance, in Louisville, Kentucky, and later as a small book, bound, designed, and printed by Carol J. Blinn of the Warwick Press, Easthampton, Massachusetts. "Downtime," "In the Cemetery High Above Shillington," "Radiators," "Religious Consolation," "Elvis and Jesus," and "Rainbow" were each separately published in limited editions by William B. Ewert of Concord, New Hampshire.

For a moment I had a view of a world that seemed to wear a vast and dismal aspect of disorder, while, in truth, thanks to our unwearied efforts, it is as sunny an arrangement of small conveniences as the mind of man can conceive.

—JOSEPH CONRAD, *Lord Jim*

To Martha

wife, adviser,
fellow American

CONTENTS

I

II

CONTENTS

III

IV

I

AMERICANA

(Poem Begun on Thursday, October 14, 1993, at O'Hare Airport, Terminal 3, around Six O'Clock P.M.)

Gray within and gray without: the dusk
is rolling west, a tidal wave of shadow
that gently drowns Chicago. Overhead,
the gray steel arches of this much-admired
architectural essay in public space
blend with gray sky and distill a double
sense of semi-enclosure, of concealment
in a universal open that includes:
the airfield with its pomp of taxiing
fresh-landed smooth-nosed behemoths;
the feeder highway sloping to an underpass
not far beyond a gray-ribbed wall of glass;
the taillights blazing ruby as autos brake
and fume with passion in the evening jam;
the silvery Midwestern sky, its height
implying an oceanic stretch of grain
whose port is this diffuse metropolis.
Without, translucent clouds; within, mute hordes
of travelling strangers, numinous, their brisk
estrangement here a mode of social grace.
No two touching as they interweave
and dodge in the silent interior dusk
beneath the mock cathedral arches, each
soul intent, each ticketed, each rapt
with a narrow vision, these persons throng
my heart with a rustle of love, of joy
that I am among them, where night and day,

mingling, make a third thing, a betweentimes
of ecstatic layover and suspension.

Women in gray jackets matching those
of men, above their taut gray skirts, and blacks
striding enlivened by the dignity
of destination, and children unafraid
of being lifted up in aluminum arms;
brightly colored pools of candy bars; the men's
room prim beside the equal-access WOMEN;
briefcases floating in a leather flock;
announcements twanging in the transfixed air
where cloudy faces merge and part again,
a cumulus of ghosts advancing, stern
yet innocent of everything but time,
advancing through me to their set departures,
through walls of gray, as nearby taillights burn
more furious in their piecemeal, choked descent.
Another fine transparency of film
is added to the evening's shining weight
of lovely nothingness, among machines.

This poem—in ballpoint, on a torn-off scrap
of airline magazine—got lost, along
with several boarding passes, ticket stubs,
and airline napkins. Now it seeks me out
here in New Jersey, on November 5th,
a Friday, in a Fairfield Radisson
that overlooks an empty parking lot.
At dusk, the painted stripes devoid of cars
are like unplayed piano keys aligned
within the drizzle that is lacquering
the Garden State. Beyond: Route 46;

an unknown mall; a stream of traffic glowing
white in the one direction, red in the other.
This poem again, its kiss of ecstasy
among waste spaces, airy corridors
to somewhere else, where all men long to be.
I strain my eyes, as neon starts to tell
its buzzing, shoddy tale; across the stream
of traffic hangs a weathered sign that spells
AMERICAN WAY MALL. The hotel room—
the shapes of luxury in cut-rate textures—
offers nothing superfluous, not even
a self-important so-called "scratchpad" near
the telephone, where travellers might write
how strangely thrilled they were to pass this way,
the American way, where beauty is left
to make it on its own, with no directives
from kings or cultural commissars on high.
It emerges, it seeps forth, stunning us
with its grand erosions of the self;
its grit of atomisms and fleet inklings
can carve a canyon or function as a clock
that wakes to tick one single tick a day.

The poem evaporates, a second time
is lost, and then a third, in your reading
here and now, which turn to there and then
as dampness overtakes, quick molecule
by molecule, the glowing moment
when God's gray fire flickers on the edge
of the field of vision like a worm of flame
that struggles to consume a printed page.

ISLAND CITIES

You see them from airplanes, nameless green islands
in the oceanic, rectilinear plains,
twenty or thirty blocks, compact, but with
everything needed visibly in place—
the high-school playing fields, the swatch of park
along the crooked river, the feeder highways,
the main drag like a zipper, outlying malls
sliced from dirt-colored cakes of plowed farmland.

Small lives, we think—pat, flat—in such tight grids.
But, much like brains with every crease CAT-scanned,
these cities keep their secrets: vagaries
of the spirit, groundwater that floods
the nearby quarries and turns them skyey blue,
dewdrops of longing, jewels boxed in these blocks.

PHOENIX

This grid of green slapped down on desert flats
relieved by bits of gray-red mountain left
like stray chunks of the undeveloped moon
calls five-lane highways streets, mile after mile
through ornate-gated, walled-off wilderness
of Spanish tile and dun ersatz adobe;
the blue-capped Western glut of space permits
some vacant blocks as long as airplane runways.

This wealth of Taco Bells and high-rise glass
will drink the Salt and Gila rivers dry
to form a golf-course universe, a garden
of imaginary blooms, a made mirage
whose web of jogging paths entraps a swarm
of retirees all struggling not to die.

ATLANTA–DALLAS/
FORT WORTH, 11:10 P.M.

The plane looked empty as I entered, but
it slowly filled, even some middle seats.
Who could be flying, so blearily late,
from hub to hub, New South to New West?

Then came a flood, ten minutes to departure,
of teenage girls, all white, most blond, in white
insignia'd sweatshirts that, plumagelike,
declared a species. "Drill team," confided

someone in earshot. "Competition in
Orlando." Sure enough, a man—a coach—
carried a spiky trophy, gilded tin.
Victorious competitors, the girls

kept pressing down the aisle with heated cheeks,
banishing our hopes of sleep with adolescent
giggling, boy-talk, camaraderie—
tongues fast as hummingbird wings, their health

an astonishment, wave on wave, shoving
into the plane's back crannies, all seats seized
by the flood (ninety-seven bodies, someone
had heard) of flesh and blood, this flushed drill team.

Slowly they quieted down. Their giggles
sank into the drone of the engines; our
drowsiness absorbed their triumphal
presence in our midst this midnight hour,

their pink membranes, their delicacy of
eyelid, lash, and tooth, their strands of hair
uncountable and glossy, the film of fat
portending womanhood, their dewy brains.

At one, mid-Texas time, another shock:
we disembarked into another mob—
parents, brandishing jackets, snacks, and names.
How fierce they seemed, frantic to claim their own!

Our ship of girls broke up on shoals of love;
the airport emptied quicker than a tide.

ON THE ROAD

Those dutiful dogtrots down airport corridors
while gnawing at a Dunkin' Donuts cruller,
those hotel rooms where the TV remote
waits by the bed like a suicide pistol,
those hours in the air amid white shirts
whose wearers sleep-read through thick staid thrillers,
those breakfast buffets in prairie Marriotts—
such venues of transit grow dearer than home.

The tricycle in the hall, the wife's hasty kiss,
the dripping faucet and uncut lawn—this is life?
No, the c.v. thrives via the road, in the laptop
whose silky screen shimmers like a dark queen's mirror,
in the polished shoe that signals killer intent,
and in the solitary mission, a bumpy glide
down through cloud cover to a terminal
where a man in armor like your own guards the Grail.

BAD NIGHT IN NEW YORK STATE

My enemy is the man (could it have been
a woman?) who left the radio alarm
in my hotel room here in Syracuse
on and set for 4:45 a.m.
At the deepest point of slumber, so deep
my brain kept trying to build him into a dream
involving, I think, a golden staircase,
a soft-rock singer flooded my sealed chamber.

Oddly, plunged into the black ocean
of the room's eruption into music, I
did not panic for more than a moment;
like a sleeper on a capsized boat, I swam,
sorting out up from down, me from him
(the loud, the terrible singer), found the light,
and killed the radio, wishing instead
to kill the man, long gone, who had murdered sleep.

THE OVERHEAD RACK

Worst of all, and most hated by me
as I sit docilely crammed into my seat,
crammed and strapped like a psychotic in restraints,
are these bland-faced complacent graduates
of business school, trained to give each other
and the rest of the poor world the business,
who attempt to stuff their not one but two folding bags
big enough to hold an army of business suits
into the overhead rack, already crammed
with travelling crap like a constipated ox's
intestine. The blond doors cannot lower,
the hats and bags of earlier arrivals
are crushed. Why don't the smug smooth bastards check
their preening polyester wardrobes and
proliferating printouts, sheaf on sheaf,
at the ticket counter, or, better yet,
stay home and attend to their neglected wives
and morose, TV-mesmerized offspring
instead of crowding their slick and swollen bags
and egos onto *my* airplane, *my* tube in space, *my*
clean shot home? Like slats of a chicken coop
overrunning with dung are the overhead racks.
If we crash, thus overloaded, the world
will yield up a grateful sigh at the headlines:
one less batch of entrepreneurs to dread.
Oh, kill, kill, kill, I think, watching the filth
strap itself in, exhaling airport beer
and nasal exchanges of professional dirt,

these fat corpuscles in the nation's bloodstream:
oh, would I were a flying macrophage
to eat them all, their bags and all, and excrete
the vaporizing lava into space!

ICARUS

O.K., you are sitting in an airplane and
the person in the seat next to you is a sweaty, swarthy
    gentleman of Middle Eastern origin
whose carry-on luggage consists of a bulky black brief-
    case he stashes,
in compliance with airline regulations,
underneath the seat ahead.
He keeps looking at his watch and closing his eyes in
    prayer,
resting his profusely dank forehead against the seatback
    ahead of him,
just above the black briefcase,
which if you listen through the droning of the engines
    seems to be ticking, ticking
softly, softer than your heartbeat in your ears.

Who wants to have all their careful packing—the trav-
    ellers' checks, the folded underwear—
end as floating sea-wrack five miles below,
drifting in a rainbow scum of jet fuel,
and their docile hopes of a plastic-wrapped meal
dashed in a concussion whiter than the sun?

I say to my companion, "Smooth flight so far."
"So far."
"That's quite a briefcase you've got there."
He shrugs and says, "It contains my life's work."
"And what is it, exactly, that you do?"
"You could say I am a lobbyist."

· · ·

He does not want to talk.
He wants to keep praying.
His hands, with their silky beige backs and their nails cut
    close like a technician's,
tremble and jump in handling the plastic glass of Sprite
    when it comes with its exploding bubbles.

Ah, but one gets swept up
in the airport throng, all those workaday faces,
faintly pampered and spoiled in the boomer style,
and those elders dressed like children for flying
in hi-tech sneakers and polychrome catsuits,
and those gum-chewing attendants taking tickets
while keeping up a running flirtation with a uniformed
    bystander, a stoic blond pilot—
all so normal, who could resist
this vault into the impossible?

Your sweat has slowly dried. Your praying neighbor
has fallen asleep, emitting an odor of cardamom.
His briefcase seems to have deflated.
Perhaps not this time, then.
But the possibility of impossibility will keep drawing us back
to this scrape against the numbed sky,
to this sleek sheathed tangle of color-coded wires, these
    million rivets, this wing
like a frozen lake at your elbow.

CORPUS CHRISTI

"Corpus," they say, as in "habeas."
Sea and land as flat as a brain-dead's beep,
though pricked with little rigs—oil, chemicals,
nobody knows for sure. The *Lexington*—
a gallant vast rustbucket redolent
of world war's canned heroics; a stale old maze
of pure-gray passageways an inch of iron
away from watery death, men drowned like moles—

is moored across from the aquarium,
where jut-jawed jewfish, jacks, and sharks,
circling and staring, illustrate some styles
of underwater survival. O stupid life!
The city's Tex-Mex half lights candles to
a Christ the Anglo half chews down with shrimp.

NEW ORLEANS

Fruit of a French scam, the New World being
one big get-rich-quick scheme, it sank its bricks
in Mississippi mud; the first dry row
received the wood of columned Greek Revival.
The whores in Storyville were kept in cribs
like pigs, naked and doomed. The yellow fever
wiped out one third the populace each summer,
but there were always more, both slaves and masters.

Now good times are the commodity marketed,
not cotton, indigo, molasses, rice.
On Bourbon Street the modern pickaninnies
tap-dance, but sullenly; the strip joints hawk
that quickly spoiled crop, flesh, night after night,
and bad rock outshouts jazz's gracious ghost.

CORINTH, MS

Two railroads crossed here, making the depot hot
property for an army that could take it.
Grant won out, and rode the rails to Vicksburg.
The little city now, uncoveted
by any side, reposes in the hope
of Shiloh's bloody glamour rubbing off
as peaceful golddust—tourist traffic. This
veranda knew the boots of Beauregard

and of Ulysses, too. What epic times
when bayonet and cannonball dispersed
the souls of country boys in gray and blue!
An iron lozenge forged to fit the wheels
that roll east-west and north-south marks the spot
a throng died for. I stood there all alone.

READING, PA

Munificence of textiles, coal, and steel
set a surreal pagoda on Mt. Penn
and filled the Schuylkill Valley with a grid
of tight-packed workingmen's rowhouses. When
the jobs moved south and malls came in, downtown—
five first-run movie houses! Pomeroy's
Department Store! soft pretzels! Santa Claus!—
went hollow, but for some Hispanic boys.

The child I once was marvelled, *City life!*—
trolleys with bright cane seats, a bustling race
of women in perms and hats, and portly men
in vests and pocket watches, a *populace*.
Now where they shopped and movies showed there is
blank blue glass: banks and welfare offices.

NEAR CLIFTON, PERHAPS

Northern New Jersey is not long on amenities.
The gas stations have no maps for sale, as if
the territory's as impossible to map
as female sexuality. The attendants
are visibly reluctant to give directions,
perhaps suspecting that even one small clue
might give the game away: the jig would be up.

One town blends into another imperceptibly,
without the grace of a field, a Lions sign,
or an Episcopal Church that Welcomes You;
such civic boasts are idle here in Clifton,
or Irvington, West Orange, or Passaic.
Humanity makes houses, houses streets,
streets traffic, and traffic trouble—a sorry state.

NEW YORK CITY

The television's just like everywhere—
the news, the so-called comedies. One feels
let down; this is a separate nation, no?
For here one speaks *inglés* self-consciously,
embarrassed to be speaking it so well
amid the toehold accents and the slurs
of knit-capped beggars whining, "Some loose change?"

This Pandemonium whose sky is like
the unfilled spaces of a crossword puzzle,
whose bad breath underground makes sidewalks shudder,
whose sheets of windows rise like thirsty thunder
above the glaze of blinding expectation—
this hell holds sacred crevices where lone
lost spirits preen and call their pit a throne.

FLIGHT TO LIMBO

(At What Used to Be Called Idlewild)

The line didn't move, though there were not
many people in it. In a half-hearted light
the lone agent dealt patiently, noiselessly, endlessly
with a large dazed family ranging
from twin toddlers in strollers to an old lady
in a bent wheelchair. Their baggage
was all in cardboard boxes. The plane was delayed,
the rumor went through the line. We shrugged,
in our hopeless overcoats. Aviation
had never seemed a very natural idea.

Bored children floated with faces drained of blood.
The girls in the tax-free shops stood frozen
amid promises of a beautiful life abroad.
Louis Armstrong sang in some upper corner,
a trickle of ignored joy.
Outside, in an unintelligible darkness
that stretched to include the rubies of strip malls,
winged behemoths prowled looking for the gates
where they could bury their koala-bear noses
and suck our dimming dynamos dry.

Boys in floppy sweatshirts and backward hats
slapped their feet ostentatiously
while security attendants giggled
and the voice of a misplaced angel melodiously
parroted FAA regulations. Women in saris
and kimonos dragged, as their penance, behind them

toddlers clutching Occidental teddy bears,
and chair legs screeched in the food court
while ill-paid wraiths mopped circles of night
into the motionless floor.

II

BEFORE THE MIRROR

How many of us still remember
when Picasso's *Girl Before a Mirror* hung
at the turning of the stairs in the pre-
expansion Museum of Modern Art?
Millions of us, maybe, but we form
a dwindling population. Garish
and brush-slashed and yet as balanced
as a cardboard queen in a deck of giant cards,
the painting proclaimed, *Enter here*
and abandon preconception. She bounced
the erotic balls of herself back and forth
between reflection and reality.

Now I discover, in the recent retro-
spective at the same establishment,
that the dazzling painting dates
from March of 1932,
the very month in which I first saw light,
squinting in quick nostalgia for the womb.
Inspecting, I bend closer. The blacks,
the stripy cyanide greens are still uncracked,
I note with satisfaction; the cherry reds
and lemon yellows full of childish juice.
No sag, no wrinkle. Fresh as paint. *Back then*,
I reflect, *they knew just how to lay it on.*

THE HEDGE

In boyhood's verdure, as if underwater,
my mother and her ancient father struggle
with a rusty brown eel, one on each end—
our iron hedge-trimmer, turned by a crank,
its two toothed levels gnashing back and forth
like the contention between parent and child.

How pink my mother's face would get! How grim
the gray of Grandpa's mustache and fedora,
its sweated brim twin to his soaked suspenders.
The hedge enclosed the wide front yard, its corners
right-angled caves where octopi might lurk
in depths of privet only a child would see.

Pride, pride of property, kept us going.
The hedge, like a leafy solid by Magritte,
had round raised intervals to reinforce
an illusion of fortress strength. In fact
we were a feeble crew; the Depression
had left us mere shadows behind our hedge.

Frail Grandma ran up a flag on Memorial Day,
on a thin tin pole. The infrequent guests
and the mailman came up a red-brick walk.
The impregnable hedge, a dry-eyed visit
some decades later told me, has vanished—
the yard, so small, barer than an old rug.

IN THE CEMETERY
HIGH ABOVE SHILLINGTON

We fifth-grade boys would thread tricolor strips
of crêpe paper through our bikes' staggered spokes,
and spiral-wrap the handlebars, and ride
in Shillington's Memorial Day Parade.
With many a halt, while gold-roped drums kept up
their thrilling, hiccupping tattoo, we moved—
the Legion bands, the shuffling vets—along
Lancaster Avenue, then up New Holland
past Mr. Shverha's movie house, where war
was cheerful weekly fare, and death more sweet
than anything we learned in Sunday school,
to this bright static ground above the town.
A granite mausoleum stated LOEB.
The nasal pieties rang hollowly
above the sunstruck flags and sharp-edged stones;
we dimly listened, kidded and horsed around
there on the grit and grass, and pedalled home.

Have fifty years gone by since last I turned
into these unlocked gates? In rented car,
on idle impulse, briefly home, if "home"
is understood as where one was a child,
I glide into this long-forgotten space
carved from a flank of bosky Cedar Top,
my tires gently crackling as I park.
The town's drab rooftops fan out from my feet.
The month is June; the seasonal flags
and potted memorial flowers still are fresh.
Sole visitor, by knocking with my eyes

on graven, polished portals set in rows
I find here what the live town lacks, some friends—
some people I once knew. Many the time,
from well within our hedged-in yard, or out
our cloudy front-room windows, did I spy
with awe and wonderment the pure-white head
of Pappy Shilling, whose father had been
the town's creator and Ur-citizen,
the subdivider of a primal farm.
So short that even a child could sense willed pride,
Pap looked too old to be a son. His cane
was ebony black; a chain of Lutheran badges
hung twittering from his blue lapel; his bangs
of cornsilk bobbed in keen-eyed childhood's glare.
He seemed a doll-man living up the street,
his house more grand than ours, and more hedged-in.
Named Howard M., he died, his granite claims,
in 1943. Eleven years
we shared on Philadelphia Avenue,
lives overlapped like trapeze artists' wrists.

Some strides away, the headstone titled BECKER
remembers OREVILLE, dead in '57.
Within my witness, Parkinson's disease
had watered his gaze to a groggy stare,
yet in his prime he was a nobleman
whose name had taken on the might of place:
Becker of Becker's Garage, its gas and grease
and oil-black floor and multitude of tools,
its blanching hiss of hot acetylene
and shelves of numbered parts and sliding doors
that rumbled overhead in tune with casters
that slid supine mechanics back and forth

like jacks of spades in a magician's pack.
My father, after school or playing hookey
for half an hour, would sit and puff a Lucky
Strike by the grease pit's edge, his run-down heels
up on the pipe guardrail in cocky style.
He owed his teaching job to Oreville, who
had swayed the school board toward the son-in-law
of Katie (Kramer) Hoyer, his wife's aunt.
ELSIE, not dead till 1970,
was one of three (like Graces) Kachel sisters,
a Kachel having wed another Kramer.
She crammed her house, next door to the Garage,
with bric-a-brac on whatnots; to a child
her knickknacks breathed of pious opulence,
as did her thickly laden Yuletide tree.
Her Kramer blood bid Elsie to be kind
to all of us, the Updikes and the Hoyers;
my humpbacked, countrified grandma was thus
our link to local aristocracy.
Without the Beckers, our newcomers' place
in Shillington would have been small indeed.

Pink polished stone adorned with mating birds
announces COLDREN—FATHER ELLWOOD E.,
SON ELLWOOD H. (his life's parenthesis
opened and closed in 1922),
and MOTHER STELLA M. Can this mute rock
be Woody Coldren, who with booming voice
and flapping arms would lead us town tots through
a storm of carols Christmas morning from
the movie house's curtained, shallow stage?
He hid the sorrow of a soon-dead child
behind a plethora of public works—

of heading up the Sunday school, of being
the borough's burgess, of bringing Noël home
full-throatedly, between a few cartoons
of Disney manufacture and the gift
of a with-almonds nickel Hershey bar
straight from Mr. Shverha's Jewish hand.
Many in this community could sing—
the German knack of *Lieder*, probably—
and I, a croaky dunce at song, was yet
enlisted snugly under Woody's boom,
within the *civitas* he cheerled on.

Here neighbors, LUTZes, lie, MARIE and BILL,
who used to sit upon their well-used porch
and nod toward our less fertile domicile.
Five sons they sent to war, and all came back.
Their stone is near-eclipsed by potted homage
—geraniums, petunias, marigolds—
a portion of their scattered spawn has paid.
Ample in form, sly in mien, this mother
of warriors was one of the neighborhood's
watchers, who made my life feel witnessed—small
but precious, set visible in her view.

But who sleeps here, nearby? Another LUTZ,
a LEWIS R., born 1928.
Can this be Looie, long-legged Looie Lutz,
who'd race down through our yard to save three steps
en route to Shillington High, where he excelled
at basketball and track, until football
bestowed a blow that left his head off-tune?
My father always called football a crime
for still-maturing bodies, and cited Looie

to prove his point. What took him to the grave
so early, speedy Looie, just four years
my senior? He became a postman, whom
I met on Philadelphia Avenue
one soft fall day, across the street from where
he used to dash, trespassingly,
along our walk, down through our arbored grapes
behung with buzzing Japanese-beetle traps,
on past our birdbath, ruffling my mother's feathers,
and through the lower hedge into the alley.
As I recall, my elders muttered in
their kitchen consultations but did not
pollute the neighborhood with a complaint,
and now that Looie's raced to join the dead
with his unbroken stride, I'm just as glad.

Few shade trees here afford the shelter for
a gloomy thought; I search the sun-baked rows
of TOTHEROs and MATZes, OLINGERs
and MILLERs, for one potent name of old,
and find it—HEMMIG, CHARLES J., known as Jack,
whose dates of '93 to '89
add up to near a century. He was
my father's boss, the lord of S.H.S.,
the supervising principal. He read
Ecclesiastes to assembly each
first day of school—"a time to cast away
stones, and a time to gather stones together."
His big head with its timid, thin-lipped smile
seemed to be melting to one side; he had
an oozy unpredictability.
He would appear within my father's class
and send my insecure progenitor

into paroxysms of incompetence.
The man had Roman hands, the senior girls
reported, and like Jupiter could be
ubiquitous, descending as a swan
in Mohnton or, in Grille, a shower of gold.
A stentor of the local charms, a genius
of local politics, he nonetheless
approved my going to Harvard, far away,
and reassured my parents that the leap
was not too daring, too Promethean.

Never shall I lie here, in trimmed green silence,
among the earners of this resting-place,
who underneath the patterned ground extend
the Shillingtonian ethos, the mild
belief that Earth's safe center has been found
beneath the heights of Cedar Top, Slate Hill,
and elevations cold ambition climbs.
I am your son; your mile-square grid of brick—
the little terraces, the long back yards—
contains my dream of order, here transposed
to an eternal scale. The flags will fade
and tatter, the flowers will turn to litter
before next May will wheel around again
its formal protest against the forgetting
that lets the living live. We were too young,
we boys on bikes, to hide the giddy bliss
of floating over people freed from need,
a field of buried guardians who bar
the pathway back with sharp-edged swords of stone.

61 AND SOME

How many more, I must ask myself,
such perfect ends of Augusts will I witness?—
the schoolgirls giggling in their months-old tans,

reviving school gossip as they hang on the curbs,
as tan as maple seeds, the strip of curbside grass
sun-parched in the ragged shade beneath the maple

that in its globular cloud of green cumulus
holds now an arc, a bulge of rouge,
held up to the bored blue sky like a cheek to kiss.

VERO BEACH BIRTHDAY

Three score three years ago, a thousand miles
north of this strand, a bundle of innards
and outward signifiers was conjured from
the reluctant loins of a Pennsylvania lass
with literary aspirations. It took
forceps to get me out, but once out, I
resolved to have what fun there was—candy,
the comic strips, the opposite sex, and golf.

Now here among retired CEOs
deposited in gated communities
whose seven-figure pastel domiciles
bespeak funereal discipline—a wealth
of wasps preserved in money's sunny amber—
the forceps tug me one notch further out.

UPON BECOMING
A SENIOR CITIZEN

March 18, 1997

The day, another grudging chill installment
of slow spring in New England, moves my mind
to Pennsylvania, the growing boy
curled above the comics amid four elders.
Early, before I scamper off to school
to hear my peers sing out the usual song
to me and Harlan Boyer, my birthday twin,
my grandfather, a sly and toothless smile
tucked under his ashen mustache, slides forward
in soft black squeaking high-top buttoned shoes
to hold out in his onionskin-dry hand
a single, folded dollar bill. Why should
this creased and meagre gift outdo in magnitude
all gifts received since then? His wallet, thin
and polished, lived a secret life. He stirred
the fire in the cellar awake each dawn
and each spring turned the vegetable garden
chocolate shovelful by shovelful.
Older even than I am now, he capped
with a country wheeze the most reflective of
his spoken sentences. A thumbnail held
near enough to the eye blots out the sun;
we hug those first years and their guardians
so close to spite the years that took away
the days of trolley cars, coal furnaces,
leaf fires, knickers, and love from above.

A WOUND
POSTHUMOUSLY INFLICTED

A stapled brown book-envelope
containing the bound galleys of
a posthumous book by a man
who once was my Harvard roommate
pricked me in the finger, painfully,
between the first and second joints.

Kit was prickly even then, in 1950,
slouching across the black-painted
floorboards of Hollis Hall, holding
out his hand in sheepish welcome. We
were mated, our troth plighted
by the deans' psychic accountants.

Both "interested in writing," both white,
both Gentile, though he had been raised
by progressive Midwestern parents
as an atheist and I by Something-fearing
Pennsylvanians as a Lutheran,
an old wooden cross in my luggage.

An unexpressible friction chafed
during our silent hours as,
both scared products of public schools,
our desks a stride apart, we strove
to make the grade, our gooseneck lamps
glaring into the assigned pages.

Love, of a kind. He cleaned up the mess
when I returned blind drunk, throwing up,

from my *Lampoon* initiation.
In beds side by side, we improvised
musical comedies and, bored at last,
suppressed the rustle of our masturbation.

He used to worry about losing his hair,
yet kept a head fuller than mine.
When last we met, after a cooling-off
of thirty years or more, he was sweet,
and looked at me as if I had amused him
all along, while we lived our lives—

our ponytailed, bluestockinged wives,
plucked fresh from the college stacks;
our quartets of children, engendered
as if by quota in some square world
of Eisenhower normalcy;
our careers and affairs, if any.

He had become a learned grump, and I
a literary Mr. Sunshine.
I resisted reading his books, and he
could not have found much time for mine.
Yet still, Kit, to reach out and stab me
this way, from beyond the grave!—

your first overtly hostile act,
not counting the sulks you could throw.
My naïve faith exasperated you.
I played bad golf all yesterday,
my finger sore and hurting just where
the grip is supposed to rest.

ON THE NEARLY SIMULTANEOUS DEATHS OF HAROLD BRODKEY AND JOSEPH BRODSKY

January 1996

I can't say either man was lovable,
at least by me, but both had bravery,
a passionate wish to push their versions through,
and my belief that words can save your life.
Harold I met when we were very young
and new to print; he seemed carnivorous
and apt to be confusing, as a friend;
his cleverness, I judged, would eat up mine.

Josip I first heard about in Moscow,
he a poetic outlaw, I a guest
of the loathsome Soviet state; in Washington,
at some posh conference, he gave my warm
hello a fishy stare and most limp hand.
How odd they died, these Brods, so close together,
their births ten years apart, and half the globe.
The competition thins; so does my blood.

ONE TOUGH KERATOSIS

My hands have had their fun, and now must suffer.
A wealth of sun, especially on the right,
un-golf-gloved hand, pays dividends of damage:
white horny spots, pre-cancerous, that grow
until the squinting dermatologist
hits back by spraying liquid nitrogen,
which stings like a persistent, icy bee.

One spot especially fascinated me—
a trapezoidal chip of cells gone wrong
between my wrist and thumb, in vexing view
whenever I wrote or gestured. Blasted, it
sat up on a red blister, then a scab.
How hideous! Obsessing helplessly,
I couldn't quell my wishing it away,

and yet it clung, a staring strange bull's-eye
both part of me and not, like consciousness
or an immortal, ugly soul. I touched
it morning, noon, and night, a talisman
of human imperfection and self-hate.
The dermatologist had botched his job,
I thought; death only would unmar me. Then

it fell off in a New York taxicab.
I brushed it lightly, settling back, and felt
a kind of tiny birth-pang near my thumb.
Release! I picked up from the seat this flesh
no longer me—so small and dry and meek

I wondered how the thing had held, so long
and fiercely, my attention. Fighting down

an urge to slip it in my jacket pocket
to save among my other souvenirs,
or else to pop it in my mouth and give
those cells another chance, I dropped it to
the dirty taxi floor, to join Manhattan's
unfathomable trafficking of dust.
A tidy rosy trace has still to heal.

OCULAR HYPERTENSION

"Your optic nerve is small and slightly cupped,"
my drawling ophthalmologist observed,
having for minutes submitted that nerve,
or, rather, both those nerves, to baths of light—
to flashing, wheeling scrutiny in which
my retinas' red veins would, mirrored, loom
and fade. "And it appears, as yet, undamaged.
But your pressure reads too high. Glaucoma
will be the eventual result if you
go untreated. What you have now we call
'ocular hypertension.'" Wow! I liked
the swanky sound, the hint of jazz, the rainbow
edginess: malaise of high-class orbs,
screwed to taut bliss by what raw sight absorbs.

TO TWO OF MY CHARACTERS

Emily, as I entered a real greenhouse,
I feared I failed to do you justice, to see
with Teddy's eyes, to smell as he would have
the cyclamens, the mums, the pithy tilth
and near-obscene sweet richness of it all,
which he ascribed to you, despite
your gimpy leg and spiky manner—
you were his hothouse houri, dizzying.

And, Essie, did I make it clear enough
just how your face combined the Wilmot cool
precision, the clean Presbyterian cut,
hellbent on election, with the something
soft your mother brought to the blend, the petals
of her willing to unfold at a touch?
I wanted you to be beautiful, the both of you,
and, here among real flowers, fear I failed.

REALITY

Displacing our plausible dream piece by piece—
the sun beneath the shade, the bedside lamp,
the saliva-moistened pillow—it asserts its rights
gently, certain of its ancient ground.
It knows it must prevail, though we turn
away into the blankets again, and drink
deep for minutes more of that alternative
where the unreal prevails and heals our sores.

Reality like a mild but inflexible mother
stands waiting in the wallpaper and the view
worn thin in the windows by blind seeing.
The bed will not make itself, the teeth will rot
unbrushed, the bladder's ache cries for release,
the world prates its promises and stale laws.

DOWNTIME

Waiting for Tom, the boy who can fix my computer if
    anybody can,
I observe how the minutes, emptied of content,
ooze past like transparent microörganisms,
in magnification's slow motion. I have time
at last to consider my life, this its stubby stale end—
whither, and wherefore, and who says?
But I fail to. I look out the window again.
A wisp from the woods announces that my neighbor is
    burning brush.
Wind tugs the rising plume this way and that,
a signifier that doesn't know its mind.
My desktop is cluttered, but what
can be discarded utterly with certainty
of its not coming back to haunt us from the kingdom of
    the lost?
My wife no longer acts like a mistress,
but surely I am too frail to seek a mistress;
passé the pink salmon's slick effortful flipping
up the icy, carbonated cataracts.
Is there anything to write about but human sadness?
Even if there were, I couldn't write it today.
My neighbor's smoke has stopped rising; his fire, too, is
    down.

III

TO A SKYLARK

Upon the lonely links, above the abundant rough,
you mount with ragged, insistent song
heavenward, far heavenward, then fall,
by staged descent, seeking a level of air
that sets your spirit off to best advantage—
a most congenial perch in breezy emptiness,
from which you sink, aflutter, to a lower,
there trembling like a leaf on thread-thin stem.

Some spot on earth holds you, some phantom nest
that roots your flighty, singing vertical.
Like cries of a crowd of children unseen,
your lone song floods the grass-floored void. I am rapt,
lifted from my earthbound plight—my life, my game—
and freed by empathy with sheer blithe being.

MARINE HOTEL, NORTH
BERWICK, SCOTLAND, MAY 1998

On the hotel-room telly, Bing and Grace
and Frank—all dead, yet here so young—in *High
Society*, a parable of how the rich
are truly better. "True Love" makes me cry.

Around me, dampness, golfing togs all soaked,
even the Dryjoys wet, wool sweaters rank
as sheep, their originals, and the sea
foaming beyond the windswept, rainswept links.

I fought for double bogeys with my life,
battered and blinking, mocked by the mouthing,
needy caddies, bitter to be out.
Scotland, where even the parson in his manse

hangs fire in predestination's kiln,
where walls' lee sides alone keep dry, where banks
built thick as mausoleums guard the tills
of a land whose single luxury is gorse.

Here, Hollywood—blue Fifties Hollywood—
this Sunday afternoon is saccharine
in tepid tea so steeped it's dark as tar.
I knew "True Love" would make me cry. Sweet Grace,

her lovely china jaw, her fake accent,
and Bing, his bouncy syllables, his ears:
they perished far from home, one after golf
in Spain, the other on a Monaco curve.

Now Frankie, too, with heavy hoopla, gone.
Yet here they are, blue-tinted to beguile
this long Scots afternoon of drying out,
of readying myself for death with tears.

PRAGUE, AGAIN

First seen in '64, a city then
of spires and malaise, with glints of jazz
and beatnikism in the people's gloom,
Prague in these more than three decades has changed.
Benign stone ogres of the High Baroque
still smile through soot and gilt, black steeples still
sprout lesser steeples, domes still hold trompe-l'oeil
Ascensions like tea leaves in cupolas
of skyey blue, but all is freshened up,
for sale. The trolley's squeal has been retuned
for tourist ears; American voices haunt
each archway. Hapsburgs, Hitler, Russians — now
the sleek brigades of Benetton and Kmart
besiege the Castle and its phantom lord.

THE WITNESSES

From Anne Frank's house in Amsterdam
(steep hidden stairs, and some unfurnished rooms,
and, in a case, a child's small, tartan-covered
diary) to the synagogue in Prague
where, in a ceremonial hall once used
for cleaning Jewish dead for burial,
drawings by children held at Terezín
are on display, the horror speaks in terms
of interrupted innocence. The dead are dead;
the guards, administrators, torturers,
and railwaymen have gone to hell for good,
and underfoot there lies atrocity
so vast that every forest voice was stilled
but these, of hatchlings wakening at night.

PIET

How strange to see an arrow-straight career!
Trees, the attempt to do the branches justice
in honest Dutch style, led him, twig by twig,
into the net of the rectilinear,
of crosses and dashes and then thick frames
for colors prime and pure as chalice jewels,
panels of heaven blazing between girders;
he believed the world could be sublimated.

Things and scenes no longer troubled him;
a square tipped onto its corner was all
he needed grant the cockeyed real until
Manhattan greeted his exile with jazz,
with boogie-woogie and a grid of streets
that proved his dream to be (bull's-eye!) the fact.

BEAUVAIS

Gigantic spiky head without a body,
supremely soaring choir without a nave,
its grand truncation foretells modern beauty
and marks the last reach of the Middle Age,
the place where the impossible refused
to come when called, by merry limestone masons
chipping a song to the Virgin, and truth
of gravity outdid the builders' patience.

For twice it partly fell—a vault, a spire—
and reconstruction, balked by plague and war,
confessed surrender to an even higher
pull, or sway: the shifting suck of culture.
The burghers put their money elsewhere, where
it counted, leaving God His vaults of air.

TWO CUNTS IN PARIS

Although stone nudes are commonplace—some
    crammed
two to a column, supple caryatids,
and others mooning in the Tuileries—
the part that makes them women is the last
revelation allowed to art; the male
equipment, less concealable, is seen
since ancient times: a triune thingumbob.

Courbet's oil, *L'Origine du monde*, was owned
by Madame Jacques Lacan and through some tax
shenanigans became the Musée d'Orsay's.
Go see it there. Beneath the pubic bush—
a matted Rorschach blot—between blanched thighs
of a fat and bridal docility,
a curved and rosy closure says, *"Ici!"*

We sense a voyeur's boast. The *Ding an sich*,
the thing as such, a centimeter long
as sculpted, *en terre cuite*, in fine detail
of labia and perineum, exists
in La Musée des Arts Décoratifs,
by Clodion, *dit* Claude Michel. A girl
quite young and naked, with perfected limbs

and bundled, banded hair, uplifts her legs
to hold upon her ankles a tousled dog
yapping in an excitement never calmed:
the sculptor caught in suavely molded clay
this canine agitation and the girl's,

the dark slits of her smile and half-shut eyes
one with the eyelike slit she lets us view.

Called *La Gimblette* ("ring-biscuit"—a low pun?),
this piece of the eternal feminine,
a doll of femaleness whose vulval facts
are set in place with a watchmaker's care,
provides a measure of how short art falls
of a Creator's providence, which gives
His creatures, all, the homely means to spawn.

DEATH IN VENICE

On one of those rare streets without a view
of water, perhaps a filled-in canal,
beyond the Rialto, near the *stazione*,
a crowd had gathered around a stricken man.
A pair of young women—one kneeling to breathe
into his mouth, the other astraddle his chest,
applying CPR with frantic heaves—
labored to save his life, it seemed in vain.

In the minute or two we watched, his face,
seen upside down like some devil's, turned blue.
My wife thought they were doing it wrong,
this pair slaving like whores at their client.
"I want to ask them if they have an airway."
He was a man my age, in a proper suit,
ripe with small signs of self-indulgence,
yet not deserving, surely, this, this fate

of a street dog, in public view, too ugly
to be pitied. He vomited white stuff
into the mouth of his would-be savioress,
who spat and bent again into the attempt
to render him erect. We turned away,
embarrassed for them all, their triple failure
to rise, as in an entangled *quattrocento*
vision, above the dust, the flow of life

reversed, redeemed, religiously transformed.
Instead they cowered, tortured and contorted
like those blue figures—his face was turning bluer—

with cautionary purpose crammed into
the lower third of some church-harbored, darkened,
creased, mold-blotted, huge, ignored Last Judgment.
How will the ambulance come, we wondered,
through all that stone whose veins are dirty water?

ORVIETO

The train stopped. We stood at a taxi stand.
No taxi came. I talked my wife into
the funicular across the street. At its top
a bus came and took us to the main square.
It was late afternoon. The cathedral front,
full in the sun, suddenly loomed, a piece
of Paradise popped up like a slice of toast—
white, striped, and mosaically aglint.

The playful grandeur piety invents!
The local, late-medieval folk, amazed,
built on the square's façades long seats of stone
where men might bask in the daily miracle,
this vertical Zen garden. There we sat,
amazed, then walked the town. Its crooked streets
all ended in a view of Umbria:
hills, fields, a train, not ours, glinting toward Rome.

items in the shop, with a showy care
worthy of crown jewels—tissue,
tape, and tissue again sprang up
beneath her blood-red fingernails,
plus a jack-in-the-box-shaped paper bag
adorned with harlequin lozenges, sad
though she surely was, on her feet waiting
all day for a wild rich Arab, a compulsive Japanese.
Grazie, signor . . . grazie, signora . . . ciao.

Nor will our thing-weary heirs decipher
the little repair, the reattached triangle
of glass from the paper-imitating end-twist,
its mending a labor of love in the cellar,
by winter light, by the man of the house,
mixing transparent epoxy and rigging
a clever small clamp as if to keep
intact the time that we, alive,
had spent in the feathery bed
at the Europa e Regina.

HIROSHIMA, 2000

Jet skiers, samurai in their scowling
flourishes as they carve the river, drown
the schoolgirl chorus's dutiful song
here by the bomb-memorial fountain.

The old Industrial Promotion Hall,
like an observatory open to
the sky, remembers a proximate star,
a white-hot instant on an August morning.

And yet, a city scintillates outside
the windows of our crystalline hotel,
where perfect brides, kimonoed or in white,
get wed in droves, amid unblemished guests.

Sheer time has swallowed the rubble and heat
and blackened flesh; the planet knows no crime,
only rampant recovery, rebirth
as cruel as it is beautiful and frail.

AT THE MIHO MUSEUM

In the suavely underlit case,
my head's shadow is reflected.
Within, an Achaemenid-period torque:
cloisonné inlay of turquoise,
lapis lazuli, and carnelian,
with a pendant of horsemen battling.
Intently the artisan (sixth to fourth
century B.C.) bent into his task,
his bones beyond dust now. I bend close
to admire. My head's shadow moves
with an eyeless insect opacity;
it, too, is a phenomenon,
alive in its moment, here above Kyoto,
where I will never be again.

SHINTO

Who living would not love red, the *torii* gates
lacquered like fingernails, and how the shrines
just wait, beneath the cedars, with their stalls
peddling embroidered charms, for what to happen?
For you to make a wish: for a believer,
however weak, to step up and clap his hands,
twice, sharply, saying to the spirits, "Here
I am, look at me, my head bowed, and listen."

There is/are *kami* everywhere, but here
and there more than elsewhere. It has to do
with Nature. The emperor, a living god,
pleasures the sun-goddess with rice and wine:
hush-hush. For him, the *kamikaze* died.
The altars hold no Buddha, just a muddle,
a chair of sorts, a mirror, dull and distant,
a minimum to pray to. Who wants more?

A BRAZILIAN VALENTINE

Lady, when you pass me on the street
the air changes color, and I want
to bite your brown shoulder.

The thought of you puts stars
into the phosphorescent sea
and warms the cold meal of my life.

Come, be the harbor to my ship,
the nest to my sharp-beaked bird.

PURA VIDA

(¡Pura vida!—*Costa Rican
phrase for "O.K." or "Great!"*)

Such heat! It brings back the brain to its basic blank.
Small, recurrent events become the daily news—
the white-nosed coati treading the cecropia's
bending thin branches like sidewalks in the sky,
the scarlet-rumped tanager flitting like a spark
in the tinder of dank green, the nodding palm leaves
perforated like Jacquard cards in a code of wormholes,
the black hawk skimming nothingness over and over.

What does the world's wide brimming mean, with
    hunger
the unstated core, and dying the proximate reality?
Con mucho gusto—the muchness extends to the stars,
as wet and numerous as larvae underground
where the ants in their preset patterns scurry and
    nurture,
and the queen, immobilized, exudes her eggs
in the dark. We are far from oaks and stoplights,
from England's chill classrooms and Tuscany's paved
    hills.

For thought is a stridulation, an insect sizzling
knit of the moment's headlines and temperate-zone
    quips,
viable in the debris of our rotting educations,
that thatch where peer-groups call each to each in semes

ecosystematically. Great God Himself
wilts with a rise in temperature, a drop in soil acidity,
an unknown language, and a lack of daily mail.
The brain's dry buzz revives, a bit, as evening falls.

SUBTROPICAL NIGHT

Orion is upstanding overhead
and Venus does a dance of slow recession
with, balanced on its back, a thin new moon—
Artemis's bow, aimed straight down.
The palms don't deign to rustle in the dark,
that dark which falls with an intemperate speed
and seems a shade of silver-green wherein
the oleander blooms burn black, like coals.

So flat, this Florida has sidewalks that
seem made for wheelchairs and for shuffling steps
too old and slow to wear away concrete.
The starlight walks upon the dimpled Gulf.
The banyans widen sideways while we watch.
A Cadillac prowls by, in search of sleep.

BOCA GRANDE SUNSET

Big Mouth, FL, where all the billionaires
are pushing out the millionaires—so goes
the local joke. Sand is a dollar a grain.
Still, the sunset comes free, and clutter-free,
done with a circle and straight line. The Gulf
has given up its Caribbean tint
already and unrolls metallic breakers
in gilded flight from the sinking sore orb,

which, touching the horizon, changes form
like an invading molecule sucked oblong
at a membrane's verge. It turns barn-shape,
broad red; is half a disc, and then a tent
trembling; then less, and is doused. A gull flaps home
through bloodied skies. Event succeeds event.

IV

SONG OF MYSELF

What devil in me likes the early dark?
My wife inveighs against Daylight Saving
but I accept that what was light-filled six
is now a twilit five,
and noon has the feel of one,
and one of an hour as far advanced as two.

The time is growing short, the shadows say,
till dinner's healing candlelight. Why
am I lately so slow to heal?
A cut at the corner of my lips—
the dentist's steely fingers reopened it.

A finger I painfully smashed, right on the cuticle,
when a fast-sliding filing-cabinet drawer
closed with my mind momentarily elsewhere—
weeks and weeks later, I watch
the squarish purple two-tone wound
move slowly out on the injured nail.
Will I live to clip it off?

Our bodies love us more than our minds do.

The slit wrists of suicides heal,
the psychotic's banged skull,
the slashes of drink-mad knife-fighters—
gray welts in the elastic black skin.
My white skin is horny with sun damage,
yet still it encloses the bone.

· · ·

At night, I lie down to sleep
in a sort of cosmic sourness, the sweat of my mind.
The death-dealing quasars at the void's far rim
come visit me to share their nullity—
splendid in their case,
ignominious in mine.

God, that dwindled residue.

My mind mocks itself as I strive to pray,
to squeeze from a dried-up creed
enough anaesthetizing balm
to enroll me among sleep's tranced citizenry,
who know no void nor common sense.

Sleep is a strange city. Even
the terror there, the embarrassments—
being naked in a supermarket, and smeared with shit—
have a healing, purgative effect.
When they lift, we are grateful
for reality, terminal though it be.

Each morning I reclaim,
reluctantly at first,
the threads of yesterday,
pulling my arms from beneath the covers
to marvel once more at my hands,
five-petalled shadows in the bedroom gloom.
I take up my body and walk.

Tomorrow is the shortest day of the year,
but by some cosmic trick, some wobble
in the earth's working-out of its spin,

the sunset has already been arriving
later each afternoon—a bed
of red coals that flares up in the woods,
yet does them no damage.

The two-tone purple spot
on my fingernail is moving out,
but slowly, so slowly,
and the keratin behind it
doesn't look smooth and healthy, as it did.
All wounds are inflicted for good.

My two new tooth implants—
are they fusing to the bone?
They sleep beneath my sutured gums
like chiggers of titanium.
The dentist's drill kept slipping,
with a gnashing my skull bones amplified;
he sweated in his intensity of skill.

My face, draped in antiseptic paper and painted,
was deep in anaesthesia, so my mind
could take a detached stance as he struggled;
but then his drill went deeper
than the anaesthesia had gone,
discovering a nerve not asleep.

I grunted in alarm, in savage protest.

He had found beneath
the skin of civilized life
the unanswerable outrage, the hot coal.
When the sliding drawer smashed my cuticle

the pain was worse even than the time
the Bucklins' yellow Labrador leaped at the fence
and fell back with my finger in his teeth.

Those scars are still there,
pale fang trails,
fading and among the lesser
of the cellular atrocities
that mar the backs of my hands.

These are always in my sight, like two open pages
of a detestable yet gripping book—
unevenly scorched, pricked up in points
as of Braille spelling an unheeded warning,
my life outdoors distilled
to these dry nubs
of microscopic breakage.

Countless hours . . . except the molecular clock
was keeping count. Tires whose treads
are worn down to the underlying threads
can be replaced with new.
So, less easily, hips and teeth. But skin
there is no trading in.

Used bodies—who wants them
save Death, the great rag-and-bone man?
We are hostages trussed in our wrinkles,
blindfolded with cataracts,
handcuffed to our painful spines.

Where else to go, who else to be,
here at this intersection of borrowed hours,

this dark wobble on the distant pivot,
blurring away our earned flaws, turning our hides
as smooth as the glossy pelt of night
in the forest fed by its own shed leaves?

The shame of time . . . yet what force else
will stir the galaxies, rotate the cells,
arrange each day's fresh, healing coat
until the last, annulling one?

My skin and I have shared a life
with something else, that rides and sees.

DECEMBER SUN

December sun is often in your eyes,
springing a foliage of lashy rays
and irritating dazzle, to replace
the foliage now stripped from all the trees.
The planet rolls and tilts beneath our feet;
the tilt obscurely works to clip the day
a minute shorter; coldness infiltrates
the web of sticky seconds and we freeze.

The year! We're chained to it as to a wheel
that breaks us, but so slowly we don't feel
a thing except at sunset, or sunrise,
when shallow angles form a kind of knife
that slices through the friendly fat of days
and bares the clockwork guts that make us die.

A RESCUE

Today I wrote some words that will see print.
Maybe they will last "forever," in that
someone will read them, their ink making
a light scratch on his mind, or hers.
I think back with greater satisfaction
upon a yellow bird—a goldfinch?—
that had flown into the garden shed
and could not get out,
battering its wings on the deceptive light
of the dusty, warped-shut window.

Without much reflection, for once, I stepped
to where its panicked heart
was making commotion, the flared wings drumming,
and with clumsy soft hands
pinned it against a pane,
held loosely cupped
this agitated essence of the air,
and through the open door released it,
like a self-flung ball,
to all that lovely perishing outdoors.

REPLACING SASH CORDS

It's easier to screw than to unscrew;
the heads have generally been painted in,
and the slots need to be chipped open. Then
the side strips pop free in a shower of flakes,
revealing the stained unpainted doors, secured
by two rust-whittled nails, to the chambers
where wait the sash weights, somber and inert.

The frayed cord snapped; a sash weight dropped one night
when no one listened. Here it rests, on end,
the simulacrum of a phallus, long,
blunt-ended, heavy, rough, its heaviness
its raison d'être, so rust and ugliness
don't matter, nor the dreadful loneliness
of being hung for decades in the dark.

Stiffened and dried by time, the knots
still yield to prying fingers. They are not
all alike; there were a number of hands;
most settled for a pair of half-hitches,
but some displayed a jaunty sailor's skill
and love of line, looped back and proudly cinched.
Dead handymen and householders less deft

come forth from these their upright wooden tombs
with a gesture, a swirl of rope before
they let the sash weight drop and, knocking, swing
back to its dark mute duty, its presence
known only in the grateful way a window,
counterbalanced, lightly rises to
admit the hum and eager air of day.

RADIATORS

Not theirs the stove's inflammatory drama,
or the refrigerator's frosty glamour,
or the trim, glazed *hauteur* of window frames,
but the warmth of the first, the erectness of the last.
Standing by a window, we feel on our knuckles a kiss
of heat like a dog's nudge, and remember that
the room lulls our blood not by accident but
by basement-based thermodynamic plan.

With their thick fins and many spines these cast-
iron soldiers stand at attention in the least
obtrusive corners, like museum guards,
sleepy and dull, in rooms of glowing treasure—
ourselves. Their weeping, whistling valves declare
a love of us that makes them throb and simmer;
they call out for our praise for their fidelity,
but are, cobwebbed untouchables, ignored.

SLUM LORDS

The superrich make lousy neighbors—
they buy a house and tear it down
and build another, twice as big, and leave.
They're never there; they own so many
other houses, each demands a visit.
Entire neighborhoods called fashionable,
bustling with servants and masters, such as
Louisburg Square in Boston or Bel Air in L.A.,
are districts now like Wall Street after dark
or Tombstone once the silver boom went bust.
The essence of the superrich is absence.
They like to demonstrate they can afford
to be elsewhere. Don't let them in.
Their riches form a kind of poverty.

MONEY

Money is such a treat.
It takes up so little space.
It takes no more ink
for the bank to print $9,998
than to print $1,001.
It flows, electronically;
it does not gather dust.
Like water, it (dis)solves everything.
Oceanic, it is yet as lucid
as a mountain pool; the depositor
can see clear to the sandy bottom.
It is ubiquitous and under pressure, yet
pennies don't drip from faucets.
Money is so tidy, so *neat*.

It is freedom in action: when you
give a twenty-buck bill to the cabbie,
you don't tell him how to spend it.
He can blow it on coke,
for all you care. All you care
about is your change. No wonder
the ex-Communists are dizzy. In
the old Soviet Union
there was nothing to buy,
nothing to spend. It was freedom
of a kind, but not our kind. We need
money, the dull electric thrill
when the automatic teller spits out
the disposable receipt.

BRIDGE

In my dreams I am always trying to get to the dummy—
its ledge of superior attack, its open chest of weapons,
the diamonds like stubby daggers, the clubs and the spades
short-handled maces poised to crush a trick,
the hearts dripping poison from their scarlet tips.
Yet something holds me back, some truth about numbers
inflexible and invisible, while losers pour
out from my hand, one after another,
to meet the derision of our enemies' trump
and their face cards—the supercilious queen
with her slim arched eyebrow, and the simpleton king,
his armless hand like a baby's on his sword.
Three living faces lock with mine in geared combat,
Which grinds, grinds away while we age and chat.

TRANSPARENT STRATAGEMS

(Based on an Article in Scientific American,
"Transparent Animals," by Sönke Johnsen)

To be unseen: a key to sea survival,
within that boundless and unsolid mass
where up is slightly brighter and down is cobalt
deepening to purple, death everywhere.

Here in still silence evolution has
the scope of volume and the breadth of slaughter
it needs to be inventive. Venus's
girdles, so-called, millimeters thick

but six feet long, pass jellyfish whose maws
are filmy, four-cornered food-traps betrayed
by eight red gonads. Even retinas,
retaining light, are not, therefore, see-through,

and hence *Cystoma*, a kind of roach of glass,
back-stroking slyly by, has optic discs
both huge and thin, and a needle-slender gut,
since food digesting also is opaque—

some pinlike guts are always vertical,
no matter how the creature's body tilts,
to cast the smallest shadow. Protocols
of great discretion mark the watery feast,

where ambush shares the table with deceit.
Siphonophores have stinging organs shaped

like baby fish, and when a predator
approaches these, an unsuspected bulk

engulfs it, swallowing. Gelatinous
means near-invisible, but delicate;
a passing fin can shred a filmy beast,
and scientists destroy what they would study.

Down here, the very skin can hide—refraction
indices douse reflectivity
with furtive microscopic surface bumps
more minuscule than half of light's wavelength,

while body cells secrete their fat in droplets
scaled to be overlooked. Still, we are seen
and eaten. Death knows who is here, though you
avoid display, stay home, and think clear thoughts.

MONTES VENERIS

Thanks to Magellan's radar, we
Have maps of Venus and can see,
The *National Geographic* claims,
Whole mountainscapes, complete with names.

Beneath sulfuric-acid clouds
That never lift their poison shrouds,
Heat like an oven's turned to CLEAN
Bakes Theia Mons, sere and serene.

Sif Mons, and Gula Mons, and Maat
(Or Ma'at) Mons are where it's at
For altitude, equatorwise.
Up north, on Ishtar Terra, lies

The Lakshmi Planum; right next door
The Maxwell Montes upward soar
And boast a lava peak whose crest
Out-towers Earth's Mt. Everest.

Heights innocent of snow and ice
And hikers seeking edelweiss,
They rise through hellish murk and are
Subsumed within the evening star.

RAINBOW

Short storms make the best rainbows—
twenty minutes of inky wet, and then,
on the rinsed atmosphere's curved edge,
struck by the reëmergent sun
in oversize, glorious coinage,
mint-fresh from infra-violet to ultra-red,
ethereal and rooted in the sea
seen through it, dyeing a bell-buoy green,

it has appeared. And when it fades, today,
it leaves behind on the bay's flat glaze
a strange confetti of itself, bright dots
of pure, rekindled color, neon-clear.
What on earth? Lobster-pot markers,
speckling the brine with polychrome.

CHICORY

Show me a piece of land that God forgot—
a strip between an unused sidewalk, say,
and a bulldozed lot, rich in broken glass—
and there, July on, will be chicory,

its leggy hollow stems staggering skyward,
its leaves rough-hairy and lanceolate,
like pointed shoes too cheap for elves to wear,
its button-blooms the tenderest mauve-blue.

How good of it to risk the roadside fumes,
the oil-soaked heat reflected from asphalt,
and wretched earth dun-colored like cement,
too packed for any other seed to probe.

It sends a deep taproot (delicious, boiled),
is relished by all livestock, lends its leaves
to salads and cooked greens, but will not thrive
in cultivated soil: it must be free.

JESUS AND ELVIS

Twenty years after the death, St. Paul
was sending the first of his epistles,
and bits of myth or faithful memory—
multitudes fed on scraps, the dead small girl
told *"Talitha, cumi"*—were self-assembling
as proto-Gospels. Twenty years since pills
and chiliburgers did another in,
they gather at Graceland, the simple believers,

the turnpike pilgrims from the sere Midwest,
mother and daughter bleached to look alike,
Marys and Lazaruses, you and me,
brains riddled with song, with hand-tinted visions
of a lovely young man, reckless and cool
as a lily. He lives. We live. He lives.

RELIGIOUS CONSOLATION

One size fits all. The shape or coloration
of the god or high heaven matters less
than that there is one, somehow, somewhere, hearing
the hasty prayer and chalking up the mite
the widow brings to the temple. A child
alone with horrid verities cries out
for there to be a limit, a warm wall
whose stones give back an answer, however faint.

Strange, the extravagance of it—who needs
those eighteen-armed black Kalis, those musty saints
whose bones and bleeding wounds appall good taste,
those joss sticks, houris, gilded Buddhas, books
Moroni etched in tedious detail?
We do; we need more worlds. This one will fail.

SAYING GOODBYE TO
VERY YOUNG CHILDREN

They will not be the same next time. The sayings
so cute, just slightly off, will be corrected.
Their eyes will be more skeptical, plugged in
the more securely to the worldly buzz
of television, alphabet, and street talk,
culture polluting their gazes' dawn blue.
It makes you see at last the value of
those boring aunts and neighbors (their smells
of summer sweat and cigarettes, their faces
like shapes of sky between shade-giving leaves)
who knew you from the start, when you were zero,
cooing their nothings before you could be bored
or knew a name, not even your own, or how
this world brave with hellos turns all goodbye.

A SOUND HEARD EARLY ON THE MORNING OF CHRIST'S NATIVITY

The thump of the newspaper on the porch
on Christmas Day, in the dark before dawn
yet after Santa Claus has left his gifts:
the real world reawakens; some poor devil,
ill-paid to tear himself from bed and face
the starless cold, the Godforsaken gloom,
and start his car, and at the depot pack
his bundle in the seat beside his own
and launch himself upon his route, the news
affording itself no holiday, not even
this anniversary of Jesus' birth,
when angels, shepherds, oxen, Mary, all
surrendered sleep to the divine design,
has brought to us glad tidings, and we stir.

A Note About the Author

John Updike was born in 1932, in Shillington, Pennsylvania. He graduated from Harvard College in 1954, and spent a year in Oxford, England, at the Ruskin School of Drawing and Fine Art. From 1955 to 1957 he was a member of the staff of The New Yorker, *and since 1957 has lived in Massachusetts. He is the father of four children and the author of fifty-odd previous books, including collections of short stories, poems, and criticism. His novels have won the Pulitzer Prize, the National Book Award, the American Book Award, the National Book Critics Circle Award, the Rosenthal Award, and the Howells Medal.*

A Note on the Type

The text of this book was set in a digitized version of Janson, a typeface long thought to have been made by the Dutchman Anton Janson, who was a practicing type founder in Leipzig during the years 1668–1687. However, it has been conclusively demonstrated that these types are actually the work of Nicholas Kis (1650–1702), a Hungarian, who most probably learned his trade from the master Dutch type founder Dirk Voskens. The type is an excellent example of the influential and sturdy Dutch types that prevailed in England up to the time William Caslon developed his own incomparable designs from them.

Composed by Creative Graphics,
Allentown, Pennsylvania
Printed and bound by Quebecor World,
Fairfield, Pennsylvania